This Call May Be Recorded

By: Joel Frieders
Illustrated By: Jose Garibaldi

**NOTE: put something whimsical here.
Bitches love whimsy.**

To my children Dylan, Leah, & Mason:
The most important trait
in any friend is thoughtfulness.
Pay attention and
learn that from your mother,
because she's thoughtful as shit.
Love,
Dad

To my wife Julie,
I still don't believe I'm your husband.
Marry me again.
Love,
Joel

To my friends, real and imagined:
cue Golden Girls theme
hip pop
Love,
Joel

To **Jose Garibaldi**,
Thank you for not immediately thinking I was
insane for wanting to do this. And thank you
for MURDERING the drawrings bro.
I look up to you.
I'm proud of you.
I love you. (Think, creepier.)

Chapters:

Introduction:

My name is Joel Frieders.

I am currently 36 years old.

I'm married to my best friend Julie, I call her Jules, and I worship the ground she walks on.

I have three children: Dylan is 8, and Leah & Mason are 6.

Yes, they are twins.
No, twins don't run in my family.
Yes, they do now.

I run a compounding pharmacy in Aurora, IL, USA, along with my sister Lydia, and my pharmacist parents, Larry and Pat.

Yes, I sell drugs on a street corner with my family.

We aren't a regular pharmacy. We're more of a restaurant for drugs.

We make everything from scratch. We specialize in veterinary medications, custom strength or allergen-free medicines, hormone replacement therapy, sterile eye drops, erectile dysfunction injections, treatments for auto-immune disorders and multiple sclerosis, vaginal suppositories, human/animal rectal suppositories (we are the "**suppository repository of the midwest**!")
(I made that up).

We take pride in what we do, we don't take ourselves too seriously, and we don't take insurance.

The following conversations and missives were documented soon after they occurred, and while I don't share people's names or medication names, I can assure you each conversation is at least 95% true. Normally, any fudging of the conversation is to protect people's private information.

Thankfully, we DO NOT actually record phone calls. Sometimes I wish we did, but in these instances, I just happened to write down the good'ns.

And before you find a reason to be offended: I don't document these things to make fun of people, I document these things to make fun of life, because we're all guilty of taking ourselves too seriously.

So stop that shit.

Now kindly take your FAX machine, and set it on fire.

Love,
Dad

P.S. I'm serious. Kill your FAX machine.

FAX NUMBER:

him: what's your fax number?

me: 630-8-

him: wait wait wait wait, i dont have a pen

me: ok, let me know when you're ready

him: ill call you back

me: ok

two minutes later

him: hi, i just called for your fax number

me: great what is it?

him: no, i need it from you

me: oh. ok, it's 630-85-

him: wait wait wait wait, i dont have a pen

me: ok

him: ill call you back

me: ok

one minute later

him: hi i need your fax number

me: want me to text it to you?

him: you'd do that?

me: seems easier than us doing this over and

over

him: ok great thanks!

me: what's your pho-

he hangs up

twenty minutes later

him: hi i called for your fax number and you said
you were going to text it to me

me: yes! what number can i text the fax number
to? i dont have your cellular telephone number to
text the number of the facsimile teleporter

him: do you have a pen?

me: ...

him: let me find out my number

me: ...

him: ill call you back

CUSTOMER SERVICE, BITCHES!

THEY:

her: hi i need a refill

me: great, what's the prescription number?

her: they send it to me

me: im they, what's the number of the RX im refilling?

her: they never ask for that

me: im they, who are you?

her: they send it to me. i never use a number

me: i am they.

her: it's for ____ and my ____.

me: great. do you have the rx numbers on those?

her: they never ask me for those

me: i'm they.

her: can those go out today?

me: we're still working on establishing your identity and what you would like refilled. what is your name?

her: they have everything on file.

me: ...

her: ...

me: they want to know your name.

her: this is ____ ___-___ (**the last name is hyphenated, BECAUSE OF COURSE IT IS**)

me: do they have your credit card?

her: they do. will that go out today?

me: no.

her: monday?

me: they say yes.

her: i'll have to come pick it up from them.

me: i'll let them know.

her: i'll come monday.

me: they will be ready

love,
they

i broke your hospital:

be me.

receive fax with some hospital orders on it. at the bottom it says "please email confirmation of receipt of this order"

i compose an email confirming receipt, i sign using my nom de plume, which also happens to be my real name

5 minutes later there's a response email i open that

it says "the following email is encrypted, please open html attachment to open securely" im like "ok sure, let's unencrypt this shit and get down to all of the taxes that are brass". im like matthew broderick in top gun

double click on html file
browser opens
it asks me for a password

i enter one that was totally secure bro, like it even had a whistle and handshake in it and shit

all of a sudden i get this weird error like i broke someone's internet
i close the browser like a 13 year old boy who had his mom walk in on him browsing "internets"

i go back to the email, double click on the html attachment
browser opens again

"the system has incurred a fatal error, please

contact the system admin immediately "

for some reason i felt bad about it like i did it to
it and it's broken now so it's all on me, fucking
ex-catholic guilt and shit

so i call the phone number on the fax and say
"hey Trudy (i dont know anyone named trudy,
im just using it here bro) I broke your computer
system by entering in my password"

and really quietly she says "the entire system is
down, what did you enter?"

and then i get all faux-defensive like "you're
asking me for my password? i, i, i, i dont know
what to say, i mean, protocol says i should never
share my passwords with anyone"

she giggles nervously, then asks if it was my
original password or if i was registering a new
one

i told her i have never click-communicated with
her with secure attachments and the browsers
and stuff so it was a new password

she's all quiet

she thanks me for the call and hangs up.

she calls back like five minutes later and has me
talk to their IT guy
he's obviously frazzled

i explain what i told "trudy" and he's like "this
doesn't make any sense"

i just sit there and dude's typing like benicio del
toro in that movie he was never in with all the
hackers and the war games and matthew
broderick has a cowlick and shit and the last
name del toro is fucking awesome

he asks me to click the attachment again but he
adds "carefully" before the word "click" like

matthew broderick and shit. so i oblige.

i carefully click the attachment by using just a millionth of the power i normally exude when double clicking attachments, the browser opens, it's working, i enter in the same password, it works, the password was nipple

guy sighs, and you can hear the control room behind him is silent because he's ALL THE IT in the hospital im assuming, and i heard a squeak so im assuming he reclined in his desk chair in victory and then went to go high five someone who isn't there but he's obviously relieved at my computer prowess.

he thanks me, i thank him. we disconnect.

so i get back to the task i was tasked with untasking before this entire drama unfolded.

i open the message.

the suspense is KILLING MEEEEEEEE!

it finally loads

and what does the fucking secure enrypted email attachment that shut down an entire hospital infrastructure for almost a half hour say?

"thank you!"

GOD DAMNIT TRUDY! STOP SAYING JUST "THANKS" IN AN EMAIL OKAY? YOU COULD SHUT DOWN A WHOLE HOSPITAL! AGAIN!

DEE-NIED:

him: i keep calling you for refills and the doctor keeps denying it!

me: sounds like your doctor wants you to schedule an appointment before issuing more refills

him: why don't they just refill it? i have an appointment with them coming up!

me: well, what's the date of the appointment, i can note that on the refill request form and maybe it'll help speed things along

him: i haven't made the appointment yet

me: whu- i feel so used.

him: what? no, it's just i haven't gotten around to calling them!

me: uh huh, i bet you say that to all the pharmacies

him: you're my only pharmacy i swear!

me: talk is cheap mister!

him: ok, ill call the doctor's office and make an appointment

me: promise?

him: i promise.

me: well forgive me for not being overly excited, there's a history here now

him: understood. i'll make things right. i swear.

me: mmhmm.

him: i'll be callin' ya.

me: mmhmm *taps foot*

SUPPOSITORIES ARE AWESOME:

her: im on my way now to pick up the _____ suppositories my vet ordered

me: sorry, i don't have the actual order yet, and i won't have it ready until tuesday late or wednesday early, but more than likely thursday.

her: what? that's ridiculous. why are you so slow?

me: i can understand that opinion. i just don't think it's physically possible to concoct a new formula for this particular medication that i don't have on hand, don't know if is available, but if it is available to me i would have to order it from out of state, wait for the package to ship, then receive the package, weigh out the ingredients, melt the base at a low temperature so as not to mess with the crystalline structure of the suppository base, mix the active ingredients and the suspending agent in the melted base, then carefully pour the liquified suppository and active ingredient mixture into molds that are at most 76F and then allow them to cool at 76F and then sit inside of a refrigerator for a few hours before opening the molds and ensuring that a compound that i've never made before with ingredients i've never worked with would meet my quality standards for being packaged, and then label and dispense it to you all in two hours and seven minutes.

her: you have to do all that?

me: yeah, it's what we do. i'm not saying it's difficult on my end, it's just a process that has to be followed to make sure you get what your doctor ordered and it works. and there's a holiday on monday, so that's all on obama. but i can help you, i just want to be upfront before i give you something to, you know...

her: shove up my dog's ass...

me: i was going to say that, but we don't know each other that well yet. i was going to say "rectally administer to the canine". i completely understand that 6 days seems like a long time and i'm sorry you have to wait, but maybe there's another pharmacy closer to where you live that could help you?

her: no, you're it.

me: okay, well, let me start the process and i'll call you back and take all your money

her: okay.

**BUTT DRUGS:

RECTUM?

DAMN NEAR KILLED EM!**

Humble Brag:

Just used the word "successtrogen" in a
sentence and I felt the feel where I was pretty
sure Jules's face was going to explode from
the sheer amazing I just spewed from m'front
face hole.

Goodbye, G'bye, Bye... BYE:

Just had one of those "i cant get off the phone fast enough" conversations that kept almost ending but then kept going before it almost ended again, but then when i was certain we were near the end it started up again.

BEGINNING & MIDDLE OF CONVERSATION...

ALMOST OVER...

OK, ENDING NOW...

***

me: ok, have a great weekend

him: you too, hey will this medication have any issues in the heat?

me: nope, not at all.

him: thanks joel, have a great weekend.

me: you too, b-

him: hey let me ask you something, does UPS deliver on Saturday's without an added cost?

me: absolutely not, you pay an arm, leg AND torso *chortle*

him: *chortle* thanks joel

me: thank you, have a good night

him: you too, hey does it make sense to ship it priority mail then so it might get here Saturday?

me: well, I won't ship this until Monday, so I'm assuming it won't take all week to get it up that short of a distance, but if you're asking if I know a guy who can send something back in time the answer is, again, no.

him: ok *chortle*, I'll stick with the UPS then for next week.

me: great. have an awesome weekend

him: you too joel, does this mean I'll have two refills left since I have three right now?

me: yep.

him: makes sense. take care joel

me: you too.

him: hey one last question, what time does UPS

normally deliver to my house?

me: they say by the end of the day, which means at the latest 8pm or so, but if you'd like I can send up one of my shady friends to sit outside and watch your front door with some binoculars, but that's not included in the cost of the RX and the shipping

him: *chortle chortle chortle* that's quite alright joel

me: have a good one

him: you too joel, hey -

me: *chortle chortle* yes?

him: have a great weekend

me: by the sound of it, with as many times as we've wished each other well, the only way we could NOT have a great weekend is if we keep saying goodbye and then not goodbying.

him: bye joel

me: HANGS UP AND GOES PEE

Goooooood Friday:

him: i was at your pharmacy on friday and yall were closed.

me: yes sir.

him: i dont see how that's possible.

me: what's possible?

him: how you can take off fridays.

me: we were closed for good friday.

him: must've been a good friday if yall were closed.

me: ...

him: ...

me: ...

him: ...

me: well i cant argue with you on that.

him: i thought so.

me: how long were you waiting to use that one?

him: since friday.

me: flawless execution.

him: i thought so. my wife didn't find it that
funny.

me: well im going to write it down and try to use
it next year and from here on out and i will take
all the credit as if it were of my own creation.

him: i can respect that.

Directional Waffles:

her: if im traveling east on Galena Blvd and then take a right on View, am i headed south?

me: sure

her: you don't sound very confident

me: you just asked me a question you could've answered yourself by never eating soggy waffles

her: what?

me: never. eat. soggy. waffles. north. east. south. west.

her: i've never heard that before.

me: i am extremely displeased to hear this. i feel like writing a letter to my alderman about my frustrated displeasure, but he's a tool.

her: what would your alderman have to do with this?

me: oh nothing, that's what aldermen do, they deal with questions and gripes about issues that have nothing to do with their actual responsibilities and they pass those questions on to people who actually get paid to answer actual government questions, but they also answer these other questions that google can answer because an "elected official" asked them, so our tax dollars are then paying government employees to google things we could just google ourselves.

her: ok, i'm coming up to view.

me: go soggy.

her: well, im not going to go waffles so i would have to go either never or soggy.

me: i feel such pride.

her: such pride. very waffle.

me: OH MY GOD YOU INTERNET!

her: I DO!

and then my day broceeded to get better...

Periods are for bitches:

her: hi i used to use your pharmacy but i switched because i found a pharmacy out of state that was much cheaper but now they're out of business and their products never really worked the same as yours did so now i need to have you overnight me the prescription i used to get with you but had you transfer to that other pharmacy but it's expired now and i have a new doctor and his office is only open for fifteen more minutes and the secretary is his nurse but it's also his wife and they don't have a fax machine or email so the overnight address is _____ and you have to hand write on the package that it's perishable and that they should ring the doorbell two and a half times not three because then the dogs will bark and ill annoy the neighbors again but what's the total on the medication and im assuming youll price match the pharmacy im switching from and just ship the medication now and we can worry about the payment details later but just make sure it says perishable and the thing about the doorbell.

me: the number you have reached, requires punctuation. please hang up, and call after hours.

her: hello?

i said nothing for about 15 seconds trying to compose myself and she hung up, but the following is what i really wanted to say, but immediately felt bad for wanting to say, but you guys are all internet assholes and can handle my come back bros

me: please, call us back at 5:01pm so you can leave a message and i can play it back over and over and over again just so i understand what im getting myself into by agreeing to price match anything especially something that was price

matched by another now out of business
pharmacy from out of state that made a subpar
product but you felt was a fair price BLAH BLAH
BLAH HOLY SHIT I WANT A TEQUILA

TRACK ATTACK:

her: i need to track an order i placed on monday, it needs to be here today

me: let me check tha-

her: it needs to be here today

me: ok let me che-

her: can you tell me if it will be here today?

me: i wi-

her: it has to be here today

me: OKIWILLTRACKITLETMEPUTYOUONABRIEFHOLD

her: it ha-

HOLD - ON TRUCK FOR DELIVERY TODAY

me: i'm sorry to keep you wai-

her: will it be here today?

me: i just tracked it and it loo-

her: it's not going to be here is it?

me: well, judging by what the tracking
information is telling me it's-

her: oh this is just PERFECT

me:
MA'AMI'DLIKEYOUTOLETMEFINISHASENTENCE

her: ok, sorry

me: your package is o-

her: i knew it. you can't trust anyone

me: on the tru-

her: i should have just driven down myself

me: ck for deliv-

her: this is unbelievable

me: ery today

her: ---

me: ---

her: well what are you going to do about this
mess?

me: what mess? it's on the truck for delivery
today? what else can i do for you besides ask you

to have a great evening and an amazing holiday?

her: *SIGHING LOUDLY* i don't know why i bother

me: yeah, it sounds frustrating to have a grasp of the english language but not the ability to stop and listen so one can understand it.

her: so are you going to reship the order today for delivery tomorrow?

me: no

her: what?

me: it is on the truck for delivery today

her: it is?

me: i said that at least twice. now thrice.

her: okay then.

me: you sure?

her: bye.

Man, I can't wait to get my jersey for TEAM INTERRUPT EVERYONE AND ASSUME THEY'RE SAYING WHAT YOU'RE EXPECTING THEM TO SAY THAT WILL ULTIMATELY DISAPPOINT YOU BUT WHEN IT TURNS OUT THEY AREN'T REPORTING BACK ANYTHING BUT WHAT YOU PAID FOR JUST SAY BYE

God named Luther:

her: how skinny are your boxes?

me: depends on who you ask

her: but your mail shippin boxes, how skinny are they?

me: i'd say smedium. probably two inches wide.

her: can you get them skinnier?

me: i could squeeze them skinnier, if that's what you're asking, but i can't be sure what's inside the box won't be impacted by my muscular prowess

her: no, i just have a pretty skinny mailbox and i want to make sure i can order something from you and have it fit in my box

me: did you measure your box?

her: no. but i can fit a pack of cigarettes in it.

me: lying flat?

her: what do you mean?

me: are the cigarettes lying flat, meaning is the widest part of the pack of cigarettes lying flat on the bottom of the box

her: i'll go check...

me: WAI-

ON HOLD ON HOLD ON HOLD

her: ok im back.

me: ohthankgod

her: i can't find my cigarettes.

me: that's a problem.

her: well, can't i order this without the cigarettes?

me: sure, we don't require cigarettes to place medication orders

her: but what about my box?

me: is your box empty?

her: yea, totally empty and i can't find my cigarettes

me: what do you have in reach that is not the phone we are speaking on

her: i have one shoe and a magazine from my church

me: is the magazine a regular sheet of paper size? 8.5 by 11?

her: i don't know, i'll go check

me: WAI-

ON HOLD ON HOLD ON HOLD

her: ok i found my cigarettes

me: ohthankgod

her: what am i supposed to do with them?

me: CRUSH THEM UP AND THROW THEM AWAY
AND NEVER SMOKE AGAIN

her: no, was i measuring something with them?

me: if you had a tape measure or ruler we could
avoid the smoking altogether

her: i have a measuring thingie, i'll go get it

me: WAI-

ON HOLD ON HOLD ON HOLD

her: ok, i have the magazine from church and it's
11 inches tall and 5 inches wide

me: which religion is the magazine?

her: lutheran

me: ok good

her: what does that matter?

me: it doesn't, im just two years removed from
smoking cigarettes myself and i'm thinking about
finding god to stop from gnawing my hand off
and a god named luther sounds pretty boss

her: no, god is god, the religion is lutheran,
started by martin luther

me: got it.

her: so, i'll measure my box with the magazine and i'll let you know how big it is.

me: you're going to put the phone down again aren't you?

ON HOLD ON HOLD ON HOLD

her: ok, i could probably fit about 15 of these magazines in the box

me: we didn't measure the thickness of the magazine, just the height and width

her: *beep* i'm getting another call, can you hold?

me: ohgod

ON HOLD ON HOLD ON HOLD ON HOLD ON HOLD ON HOLD

her: just had an idea, what if i had the package shipped and have the delivery man leave it on the porch?

me: i love this idea

her: excellent

me: so what's the prescription for?

her: i'll spell it "Premarin"

me: that's commercially available, you can get

that at walgreens or CVS or whatever your local
pharmacy is called

her: oh, they're right next door! do you have
their number?

me: i do not.

NOR DO I HAVE THE WHEREWITHALL TO HAVE
ASKED THIS QUESTION AT THE BEGINNING OF
THE PHONE CALL

BYE

This is RIDICULOUS!

him: i placed an order TWO DAYS AGO and I
STILL DONT HAVE IT! this is RIDICULOUS!
me: so you placed an order the day after a
national holiday, you asked that it be shipped to
your place of residence and you haven't received
it? let me check on it
him: this is RIDICULOUS!

***places gentleman on hold, kisses three babies,
finances three world wars and massages one
goose***

him: *FUMING*

me: looks like it's on the truck for delivery today

him: this is RIDICU-

me: ...

him: i guess that's all i need from you

me: ... sorry to disappoint you

him: *hurumph*

me: ...

I WANT TO TAKE A MINUTE TO APOLOGIZE TO
THE MAN WITH THE SICK ANIMAL WHO WAS
ANGRY THAT WE RUSHED AN ORDER OUT AT
HIS REQUEST ONLY TO HAVE IT ARRIVE THE
DAY HE THOUGHT IT SHOULD HAVE, BUT HADNT
CONSIDERED A SMALL BUSINESS HAD
ACTUALLY DONE WHAT HE REQUESTED AND
PAID FOR, EVEN THOUGH IT WAS THE DAY
AFTER A NATIONAL HOLIDAY AND EXTREMELY
BUSY, SO HIS ATTEMPT AT BELITTLING A
COMPLETE STRANGER WAS THWARTED BY A
SMALL BUSINESS THAT HAD ACTUALLY DONE
WHAT HE REQUESTED AND PAID FOR.

Sorry you didn't have anything to yell at me about sir. I know that feel.

This reminds me of that one time at this bar I worked at in college "The Ritz" when a friend of mine was trying to fuck with a co-worker of mine:

him: WAITRESS! THIS BURGER IS WELL DONE!

her: im so sorry sir! ill have them recook it right away!

him: NO, NO, NO! GIVE MY PRAISE TO THE CHEF, THIS IS VERY WELL DONE!

her: i dont understand you sir!

runs away crying

I CANT PLEASE EVERYONE, EVEN BY PLEASING THEM, I HAVE UNPLEASED THEM

i fail

Take my money:

her: i needed to pay for my prescription, can you help me with that?

me: ma'am, if there's one thing i can help you with, it's separating you from your income.

her: what?

me: yes, i can help you pay for your prescription.

her: ok. im holding the card up in front of the phone now.

me: ok, a little to the left.

her: better?

me: i was being sarcastic, i don't have facetime or skype or any sort of futuristic two way camera device on this landline phone, im sorry to have mislead you.

her: how's this?

me: lower.

her: good?

me: perfect. now if you can just read me the numbers on the card in groups of four, and then give me the expiration date and then the three digit code on the back.

her: *reads me numbers*

me: thanks, i'll get working on this now.

her: awesome, thanks!

never in all of my many many years of selling drugs have i experienced someone assume i could see what her phone's camera could see without any reference to being connected via facetime/ skype.

but it's only 2:05pm, there's still time to shock me bros

also, nice sweatervest bro!

This is my **PERSONAL** cell phone:

me: hello, is this ____?

him: WHO IS THIS!? this is my personal cell phone!

me: excellent! if you answered someone else's phone we'd be in quite the pickle.

him: where did you get this number?

me: you.

him: ME?

me: you.

him: ME? WHAT DO YOU MEAN ME?

me: well, if you're saying me, it means you. and me being me, and telling you you, i mean that im saying you gave me your number.

him: where did i give you this number?

me: ...uh...

him: that's what i thought, you're one of those telemarketers!

me: i'm actually returning your call.

him: MY CALL? WHAT DO YOU MEAN MY CALL?

me: well, if im saying you called me, it means my phone rang when you attempted to contact me, yet i was unavailable, so they took down your number and im calling you back about whatever it was you had called me about.

him: WELL WHO IS THIS!?

me: j-

him: WHO IS THIS!??!

me: jo-

him: TELL ME WHO THIS IS OR IM CALLING THE POLICE!

me: JOEL. MY NAME IS JOEL FRIEDERS. I LIVE AT 420 HIGHBRO LN IN YORKVILLE, IL 60560. I AM 35 YEARS OLD. I HAVE A WIFE AND THREE KIDS. I SELL DRUGS ON A STREET CORNER WITH MY FAMILY AND I REALLY WOULD JUST LIKE TO RETURN THE PHONE CALL YOU LEFT WITH ME AT 4:07PM TODAY, MARCH ELEVENTH THE

YEAR OF OUR LORD TWO THOUSAND FIFTEEN.

him: oh yea. hey, you're the bee guy! you got any honey for sale.

me: ...

him: ...

me: ...

him: ...

me: probably end of june. but check the garden faire in oswego, they stock local honey and they have amazing perennials.

him: hey thanks.

me: *sniff* sir, yes sir. *sniff*

IM GOING HOME FUCK EVERYONE

We open:

her: you guys open right now?

me: ...

her: ...

me: um, yes?

her: oh good. ill call back.

me: what? when?

her: in a little while, im not in a place where i can talk right now

me: im not even sure i know how to respond to that

her: ...

me: k bye!

her: ill call you soon

me: YES!

EYES ROLLING IN CIRCLESSESESESESES

Shipping is cheaper:

him: so what's it cost to ship my dog's medicine?

me: ten bucks

him: what about if i pick it up?

me: ...

him: ...

me: ... twenty.

him: seems cheaper to just have you ship it.

me: ...

him: ...

me: ...

him: ...

me: ...

him: well okay.

me: yes.

You'll never make it:

her: hi, im going to drive in from Joliet to pick up my prescription, what time do you guys close?

me: 5pm, you'll never make it.

her: what time do you close tomorrow?

me: 5pm, if you leave now you might make it.

her: when?

me: 5pm

her: for pick up when?

me: anytime between 9am and 5pm, monday thru friday

her: you said i wouldn't make it in time

me: well yeah, if you tried to get here today

and left now

her: what about tomorrow then?

me: if you left now you would most certainly make it

her: but you close at 5

me: we do

her: ok

... 5 minutes later ...

her: i was speaking with a gentleman a moment ago, he told me you guys close at 5

me: smart guy, yes, we do

her: but tomorrow you close at 5 too

me: yes

her: ok, thank you

I DIDNT MEAN TO CONFUSE HER, I ASSUMED SHE WAS MESSING WITH ME

SO MANY WAITING:

her: IVE BEEN WAITING OVER A WEEK FOR MY
ORDER AND IT IS STILL NOT HERE!

me: well that's just sucky, let me take a look

her: THIS IS UNACCEPTABLE!

me: it sure is, i can't imagine waiting that long for
an order, who are you? I'll start tracking on my
end

her: WHAT DOES THAT MATTER? JUST FIND MY
PACKAGE!

me: yes'm, will do, just need a name to associate
with the package so i know which package goes
with which person because there's a whole
buncha packages with names on em, and i dont
wanna reference the wrong package if it isn't

yours. i had that happen once. messy situation indeed.

her: *LOUD EXHALE* (reluctantly gives me her name)

me: ok, I'll get to tracking, can i put you on hold or can i entertain you with my breathing?

her: BREATHING IS FINE

me: *tracking tracking tracking* *breathing breathing breathing*

her: *heavier breathing than myself*

me: looks like it shipped on the 2nd and was delivered on the 6th. is there a milk box it could be stashed behind?

her: I DONT EAT DAIRY

me: me either, woooooooo boy *makes popeye pipe toot noise along with fist toot/pull*

her: I DONT HAVE IT, WHERE IS IT?

me: well if there isn't a milk box it's hidden behind, could it be at the post office?

her: IT'S A PO BOX.

me: oh. well then let me get you the number for your local post office

her: I HAVE THAT NUMBER

me: well, shall we call them together and get to the bottom of this?

her: WHY DIDNT THEY CALL AND TELL ME MY PACKAGE WAS HERE?

me: i take full responsibility.

her: THIS IS UNBE- *hangs up*

me: if you aren't doing anything later... i got these cheeseburgers...

her: *dial tone*

me: ma'am? maa'aam? MA'AM? MAAAAA'AMMMMM!!!!!!

#missedconnections

Are you open now?:

her: what time are you open to today? 5?

me: ye-

her: are you there now?

me: ...

her: hello?

me: ye-

her: what am i saying, of course you're still there

im talking to you and it's before 5

me: TO LEAVE A MESSAGE, PRESS 3.

her: *boop*

me: YOUR TOTAL BEFORE SHIPPING IS FOUR

HUNDRED AND SEVEN DOLLARS TO ACCEPT,

JUST HANG UP. TO CANCEL, PRESS adsjfaja

her: NO NO NO NO NO

me: i'm kidding, we're here until 5

her: what?

me: TO LEAVE A MESSAGE, PRE-

her: *click*

**three seconds later **

her: are you guys open?

me: (SERIOUSLY TEMPTED TO CONTINUE THE CHARADE) yes ma'am, sure are.

her: i could've sworn i called you a second ago but i got this weird thing saying i had spent 400 bucks

me: hmm, crazy

Drugs for money:

i almost just let myself go over that imaginary line i pride myself in normally tiptoeing around. i could tell this particular woman wanted someone to yell at, probably due to things outside of my control or understanding, but while at first i wasnt up for the challenge, her need to fight someone was very difficult to ignore, and it took every ounce of my being (7oz bros) to not tell her to fuck right off. but i did what my daddy taught me, i interjected complete ridiculousness inside of her tantrum-directed-at-anyone and calmed her the fuck down. and while it angered her to be unangered, i think we both got what we wanted out of this interaction.

her: did you send my order yet? i needed it
today!

me: no, looks like we are waiting on payment.

her: what! this is ridiculous!

me: i agree. paying for things does seem to get in
the way of most things.

her: i need that order TODAY!

me: i agree.

her: well if you agree why didn't you ship it!??!

me: well, standard operating procedures instruct
us to receive payment before sending out orders
to strangers. sort of a "you give me money, i give
you drugs" scenario. keep in mind, we're like a
restaurant for medicines, not a grocery store
where everything's already made. kind of like
placing an order for a burger.

i would love to give you this burger, it's delicious,
but it requires payment up front, as me making
this burger and it potentially going uneaten
would impede the swiftness with which i cook
another burger for the paying customer with an
open salivating mouth behind you.

her: well, cancel the order!

me: i would, but i cant. i never started an order because an order would mean that all of our ducks were in a row. i am missing ducks ma'am, do you have ducks? to be an order i need a duck.

her: so you're admitting it! you never made it!

me: correct. i also never made my son the "poached egg surprise" i promised him. but, just between me and you, the surprise is i wasnt going to make him a poached egg anyway.

her: what are you talking about!

me: well, i get the feeling youre having a bad day and are on the hunt for someone to yell at, and while i understand you forgot to call back with a credit card yesterday, the only way i can get you what you need as soon as i am humanly capable, is for you to give me the duck i need to put in this row, and rather than have you yell at me like im intentionally stressing you out, im finding every opportunity to say things that will hopefully convince you to stop yelling at a random stranger that just wants to make these delicious suppositories for you.

her:...

me:...

her:... it's a visa.

AND THAT MY FRIENDS, IS HOW YOU DISARM A
WOMAN HELLBENT ON SHOVING HER FOOT
DOWN YOUR THROAT.

"ass gaskets":

her: do you guys sell the paper toilet seat covers
that you put on the seats of toilets to... uh...
what's the word im looking for...

me: cover them?

her: THAT'S IT!

me: not at all

her: are you sure?

me: let me put you on hold and double check

PLACES ON HOLD

me: yep, still no. sorry.

her: darn

me: darn indeed.

Your cat. Has a behaviorist:

her: my cat's behaviorist wrote the prescription.

me: ...

her: it's for her behavior.

me: ahhhhh

her: we are hoping this will improve her behavior

me: this medicine is for treating an infection

her: well the infection is obviously affecting her behavior.

me: it would definitely affect mine, remember, this is an animal-judgement free zone

her: well thank you

me: INSERT PICTURE OF MY EYEBALLS

sigh:

her: *sigh* hi, *sigh* i left a message over the
weekend and im following up on it

me: cool, let me go look for the message and see if
there's an order already in queue

her: *sigh*

PLACE HER ON HOLD

me: yeah im sorry i am not seeing anything so ill
take the order from you now

her: *sigh*

me: whenever you're ready

her: *sigh*

me: do you need to call me back? you're sounding
kind of breathy.

her: *sigh* no

me: ...

her: *sigh*

me: is there anything i can do?

her: *sigh* i just wish you had called me when you didn't get my message

me: *sigh*

her: i mean, i left a message. you could have called that you didn't get my it

me: i apologize that technology burped, i accept full responsibility for that, but if we didn't receive the message i wouldn't know you had left a message, so to leave you a message or call you about the message we didn't receive, well, im just not sure how that would work

her: but you have the message now?

me: no, technically i know you left a message, but without the message i just don't know what the message said. can i take it from you now?

her: i left it on saturday

me: yeah, totally understood. can you repeat the message you left on saturday then so i can get working on your order?

her: *sigh*

AND THIS CONTINUED FOR FIVE MINUTES UNTIL
I SAID: "if you were, say, living life last saturday,
and you had dialed my number and were about to
leave a message, what would the message say ya
think?"

wipes hands

drops phone

A doctor doctor:

him: you guys fill prescriptions for prescriptions there?

me: yes sir. we also fill prescriptions for prescriptions.

him: is that right?

me: ...

him: so do i need a prescription to get something filled then?

me: sounds like you've done this before.

him: heh heh heh. can doctors write prescriptions?

me: medical doctors yes, I don't want to see any prescriptions come through from a professor of

English if you catch my drift.

him: well that's going to be a problem.

me: i'm sorry to hear that.

him: i'll have to call you back.

me: i will look forward to your call and hope to build a beneficial business relationship built on trust and mututal respect.

him: as do i.

me: then it's settled...

EYES ROLLING IN CIRCLES EMOJI

My kids are smarter than their dad:

dylan: DAD! MASON CALLED ME STUPID!

me: are you?

dylan: NO!

me: then what does it matter what someone else says about you?

dylan: *pouting* it doesn't.

me: you think it matters what people say about me?

dylan: like the lady at target that pointed at you and said you were a-

me: yes, dylan.

dylan: and that guy at the festival that said your ideas about-

me: YES, dylan

dylan: and the newspaper article that said y-

me: YES, DYLAN.

dylan: and the lady in the parking lot who didn't see you backing up and honked and then started-

me: OK THANK YOU, YES. YES, THANK YOU FOR UNDERSTANDING THIS LIFE LESSON NOW PLEASE SHUT THE FACE YOU ARE SPEAKING FROM...

WHY MY KID GOTTA UNDERSTAND SHIT

Dat road tho:

Me *listening to voicemail in car through loudspeaker of angry human who had to sit for fifteen minutes on cannonball trail yesterday while two steamrollers rolled steam over areas that needed rolled steam from steamrollers whose main responsibility is to roll steam*

Me: *calls back angry human with smile on face*

Angry Human: hello?

Me: Hi, calling you back from yesterday, you left a voicemail regarding cannonball construction congestion?

Angry(?) Human: Yea, well I just got home from taking my kid to school and, the, uh, the uh, the road is great.

Me: I just took that curve at 35mph, in the rain, and giggled. I feel like I'm wearing new socks.

No-Longer-Angry Human: Yea, wow.

Me: Sorry construction took two days there. Hoping the rest of it is easier when they finish the driveways.

Human: Oh, no worries, kinda sorry I left that message.

Me: I deleted it before you finished.

Human: So you didn't hear the end?

Me: Maybe.

Human: ...

Attention, jesus:

her: is this going to anyone's attention?

me: jesus

her: last name?

me: h. christ

her: is that really his name?

me: WHO DO YOU SAY THAT HE IS?

her: what?

me: WHOOOO DO YOU SAAAAAY HE ISSSSSS?

her: what?

me: im going to start quoting ghostbusters if
we don't hang up, just send the goods to jesus
h christ and put a bird on it.

her: yes sir.

I judge you:

you have to question the sincerity of people who don't scream WOOOOOOOOOOOOO on the initial voyage down an unfamiliar waterslide. WHAT THE FUCK IS WRONG WITH YOU? THIS IS WHERE YOU WOOO, REGARDLESS OF WHETHER OR NOT YOU HAS A SCRIPT BRO. cmon bros.

wooo on the waterslides bro

Waterpark lifeguard checking out my bacon leg tattoo:

him: is that bacon?

me: do you want it to be?

him: kinda.

me: then yes, it's bacon.

him: HUGEST GRIN IVE EVER SEEN ON A LIFEGUARD GETTING READY TO PUSH ME AND MY DAUGHTER DOWN A SLIDE.

We don't carry that, no:

him: do you guys sell

Arinthrocaricafigurnificansiplis?

me: no.

him: did you even look?

me: no. but sir, I can pronounce words that haven't been pronounced since the dawn of modern speech, I can assure you that the word you just said to me is either a mispronunciation, you're making that up, you are rickrolling me, or that is in fact the latin term for "the roll that is rick".

him: they say it's for arthritis and candida.

me: who is "they"? I say I'm for world peace and tortilla chips, and I assure you I exist, but in this world there is no such thing as

Arinthrocaricafigurnificansiplis.

can you spell it?

him: no.

me: so you're just pronouncing it how you

assume it's pronounced? Who told you about this

and do you trust them?

him: Joel, it's me Rick.

me: YOU ARE SUCH A DICK.

I understood:

A woman just read her credit card number to me
while asking questions in between numbers.
I'm celebratory because I got the whole card
number correct, but also slightly ashamed
because I wasn't listening to her questions, which
were regarding differing strengths of the
medication she was paying for. Had I been able to
take down the card number while digesting the
questions on strength, I'm sure my mind
would've looked a little something like what Little
Man Tate sees in his head huh?

Credit card school:

dear people of earth,

when providing (or BROviding bro) your credit
card over the phone to another human who may
be selling you pizza, taking a down payment on
your cable installation, or accepting your pay off
of your student loans, or in my case fucking
drugs bro, here are some things to keep in mind:

*read the numbers as numbers in groups of four,
and keep it moving.

*dont wait for me to grunt after each grouping of
four numbers. if i wait long enough for you to
continue and i grunt, im probably grunting over
your saying the next four numbers bro

*don't say "four thousand and twenty seven",

don't say "forty twenty seven" or even worse "forty two seven", dont say "four hundred and two seven, don't say "four oh twenty seven", just fucking say four zero two seven bro.

*dont stop midway through the third bunch of four numbers to say OH, IT'S A VISA.

I KNOW THAT BRO. if your card starts with 4, it's a visa. if it starts with a 5, it's a mastercard. a 3? a fucking amex. 6? discover bro. this is not new information.

nothing in life is that difficult. except attempting to take down a credit card number from someone who believes it IS indeed difficult and DOES need to make it seem like they're explaining the molecular make up of the feces of the monarch butterfly (they do poop bro, cmon).

these are the people who spend 15 minutes ordering a beer at a festival with two beer options.

these are the people who can't decide between

one pizza or the joey special. (TWO PIZZAS BRO)

these are the people that will wait at a stop sign
for you to stop, when you are clearly stopping,
only to gas it, BRAKE! then gas it, BRAKE! and
then slowly creep through the intersection while
glaring at you when you didn't make any attempt
at taking their turn, but holy shit as they glide
through the intersection it would be great to
somehow pull in front of them, although it would
be physically impossible.
these are the people who assume because they
haven't thought thoughts before, that they are
the first thinkers to have thought the thoughts.

THEY THINK ALL OF THE THOUGHTS.

im done. *waves*

INTERRU-:

her: i need a prescription refilled.

me: great, what's the na-

her: can you help me with that?

me: sure, what's the na-

her: what do you need from me?

me: can i have your na-

her: i have an RX number

me: can i have the na-

her: do you want that number?

me: can i have the na-

her: what do you need from me?

me: can i have your na-

her: just the number?

me: name?

her: will the number work?

me: NAME!

her: just let me know

me: NAME?

her: do yo-

me: NAME?

her: what?

me: let me know when youd like me to talk

her: ok, talk

me: what is your na-

her: the number is-

me: name

her: what?

me: *puts woman on hold*

breathes

kindly asks technician to take the phone call

thirty seconds later

tech: MA'AM, MA'AM, MA'AM, CAN I HAVE
YOUR NAME?

me: *smiles*

The fax machine is reliable:

monday: 11:09am

her: did you get my fax? i sent it again

me: no. do you just want to tell me what youre
trying to fax and i can write it down? this is what
faxes used to be, mouth to ear to paper and such.

her: ill try again

me: wai- *CLICK*

monday: 12:23pm

her: did the fax come through yet?

me: no. do you just want to tell me what youre
trying to fax and i can write it down?

her: ill try again

me: wai- *CLICK*

monday 1:46pm

her: did my fax arrive?

me: no. do you just want to keep faxing me and then calling me to see if it came through and when it doesnt, instead of just telling me what youre trying to fax me, you just keep trying to do the same thing that isnt working, over and over?

her: yep, ill try again

monday 2:15pm

her: did the fax come through okay?

me: no

her: this is aggravating

me: not to sound insensitive, but you can just tell me over the phone what you're trying to fax and maybe i can save you some time or even just take the message over the phone

her: i think id rather try again

monday 3:34pm

her: did you get my fax?

me: I DID!

her: great!

me: im lying, i havent received anything

her: can i just tell you what im trying to fax you over the phone?

me: YOU CANT BE SERIOUS! EVERYTHING MUST

BE FAXED!

her: damn!

me: im kidding, what are you trying to fax

her: it's an invoice for the GMC service we perfo-

me: no one here owns a GMC

her: it's one of your service vehicles

me: oh right the service vehicles

her: wait

me: im waiting

her: i think ive made a mistake

me: just one?

her: *click*

AND THUS COMPLETES A DAY IN THE LIFE OF A
WOMAN TRYING TO SEND A FAX THAT WONT GO
THROUGH TO A PLACE SHE WASNT EVEN
SUPPOSED TO BE FAXING SOMETHING TO IN THE
FIRST PLACE AND RATHER THAN FINDING THIS
OUT BEFORE LUNCH, SHE'S ALREADY ENSURED
THE REST OF HER DAY IS POO BY NOT USING
HER MOUTH HOLE.

everyone, just use your mouth hole.

This person is white, I guarantee it:

her: hello i need to get a prescription reordered.

me: great what's the name the prescription is under?

her: i'm not sure if it's my maiden name or married name

me: ok, let's start with either

her: i'm also not sure if you have my name or my abbreviated name as the first name

me: is your name Janice?

her: no

me: is your name Tameeka?

her: no

me: JEFF! your name is Jeff!

her: no.

me: ok, well i'm out of ideas Joan

her: try _____.

me: nothing, i can also look you up by your prescription number

her: ok, it's 209892384902340

me: yeah i don't have any rx's with that prescription number, i'm sorry. is there a number on your label or invoice that has RX in front of it?

her: i don't have a label or invoice with me

me: ok, what about your birthday?

her: i was born in a leap year

me: ok, well what's your prescription for, when was it last filled, and who is the doctor who filled it? i can run some quick reports and find out who i say you are and get you what you say you need refilled.

her: i don't know what it's called

me: ok, what's the medication for?

her: i don't care to explain

me: understood.

her: maybe i can just give you my name?

me: excellent.

her: (NAME GIVEN)

me: here you are. and you're calling for a refill on (RX NUMBER). ok, ill work on this immediately, is the credit card we have on file current? (**I KNEW I SHOULDN'T HAVE ASKED THIS**)

her: gee, i don't know if you have my new card or my old card.

me: would you like to give me the card you have in your possession that you know to be current so as to avoid any further delays in the processing and filling of your prescription?

her: does the card you have end in ****?

me: no.

her: does the card you have end in ****?

me: no.

her: does the card you have say CHASE DEBIT on it?

me: i don't have any way of knowing what the actual card says on it, just the last 4 digits and what type of card it is, unless you're checking out with that credit card in our pharmacy

her: ok, when will you know what card you have?

me: i have the card ending in ****

her: i don't have a credit card that ends in that. where did you get that number?

me: i would assume it was provided to us at the time of the last fill, possibly by you or a member of your family with access to your billing information

her: well, i'm not comfortable giving you a different number if you cannot tell me who gave you that other number

me: ok

her: so what do we do now?

me: would you like to speak with someone else here and give them the credit card?

her: sure that would be fine.

me: ok please hold.

place her on hold

JESSICA! PHONE CAAAAALLLL!

WHAT THE FUCK IS HAPPENING IN MY LIFE THAT MAKES THIS SHIT HAPPEN ALL THE TIME?

Uh oh, that sigh sounds bad:

me: hi, i got your refill request and see you'd like a two month supply of your medication. i just wanted to let you know there is only one month remaining on the prescription so i've called your doctor for more refills so i can fill the two months for you.

her: you guys are unbelievable.

me: good unbelievable or bad unbelievable?

her: every time i order there's a problem with what i've ordered. how come every time i order you just don't fill the order and send it to me?

me: **quietly looking at her rx history and seeing this is her first ever rx with my pharmacy** gee wilickers ma'am, i'm sorry. let me take a peek and see what i can see. it looks like the last time

we filled a prescription for you was 11 months
ago and it looks like it was a rush order and you
picked it up three days after it was filled and
marked RUSH ORDER! PICK UP IN ONE HOUR.
was there something my computer isn't telling
me that i can address with my staff?

her: *sigh*

me: uh oh, that sigh sounds bad.

her: ...no.

me: okay, i'll call you when the order is ready for
pick up then.

her: it's just-

me: ...

her: every time i've used your company there's a
hold up.

me: i understand.

her: every single time.

me: i understand. what was the hold up the one
time?

her: i showed up and my order wasn't ready.

me: my apologies. i know you already understand
that we aren't a traditional drug store and that
everything is made to order. so if we received

your order and did not have it ready when we
said we would, i apologize.

her: i had hoped that this time around it would be
different.

me: alas, it is not. i have disappointed you.

her: *sigh*

me: is it okay if i call you after your doctor calls
in refills and i make your prescription then?

her: *sigh*

me: *sigh*

her: *sigh*

me: okay then, have a good day.

Brand NEW:

10:35am

her: my doctor's office is going to call you with new prescriptions, call me when you receive it.

me: okie dokie.

11:55am

doctor's office calls in new prescriptions on two medications that still have refills remaining on two other prescriptions.

12:00pm

i call her back. i have to leave a message.

1:45pm

she calls me back.

me: hi, so the doctor's office called in more refills

on the prescriptions you still have refills on. was something supposed to change?

her: no i just needed new prescriptions.

me: gotcha. well those old, still current, prescriptions have refills, and these new prescriptions now have refills, so next time you can call me for a refill instead of the doctor for a new prescription and it won't require all of this back and forth.

her: ok, why don't you fill the stronger of the two and send it to me.

me: okie dokie.

not even five minutes later

her: hi i just called about having my new prescriptions filled.

me: yea, i spoke to you just a minute ago, how can i help?

her: can you fill the other prescription that was called in too?

me: absolutely.

her: can you send it to me then?

me: of course.

her: thanks.

me: you're quite welcome, talk to you in a few minutes

her: ha!

MORAL OF THE STORY: i dont think this particular lady likes refilling things. i think she just likes new prescriptions. because she has multiple new prescriptions all with refills remaining, all for the same thing.

some people just have fucking standards, and refills are for peasants.

Automated refill line:

him: yeah, ive been using your automated refill line and i still haven't received my medication

me: we don't have an automated anything around here. what number were you calling?

him: this one

me: what did you do when you were presented with an option?

him: i hit the number to leave a refill and then i typed in the refill number

me: so you're the guy leaving the beeps

him: can i give you the number so it can get refilled?

me: yea of course, i'll fill it now

him: BEEP BLOOOP BEEP BLOOP BLEEP BOOP

me: hey man, just tell me the number

him: ah, my bad BEEP BLOOOP BEEP BLOOP
BLEEP BOOP

me: nah, nah, nah, with your mouth

him: oooooooooooooooohhhhhhhhhhh ******

me: i don't have any record of that prescription
in my software, let me look you up by your name

CLICK

i wonder what happened.

Dat math:

me: the price is $53.

him: how can i get a bigger discount on the medication?

me: well i could raise the price.

him: how much would the discount be then?

me: well...

him: i just don't want to pay full price for it

me: ok, i can raise the price by 20% and then give you a discount on that

him: awesome, thank you

me: you're serious?

him: i appreciate it!

me: me too!

YAYsayer:

...and then i turned a naysayer into a YAYSAYER!

him: hi, id like to cancel a prescription i had filled
a few weeks ago
me: well, if it was filled a few weeks ago it can't
be cancelled. technically you can only cancel
something that hasn't been filled yet, otherwise
we're just throwing drugs out the windows and
these windows don't open
him: well i would like to not have it filled a few
weeks ago
me: whuu, marty?
him: what?

me: sorry, that was my passive aggressive doc brown saying let's go back to the future and cancel something that's currently made and waiting for you to pick it up

him: yeah i didn't think about that, it's just i can't get in there to pick it up

me: hows abouts i ship it!

him: THAT WOULD BE GREAT! HOW DOES THAT WORK!

me: you, me, prescription, credit card, swipey swipe, cha-ching, box, tape, ice brick, print, ship, ding-dong, hello here's your prescription, you "hell yea"

him: let's do it

me: ALRIGHT!

him: man, i'm a little excited now!

me: good! this is an excellent canine suppository! it's the most canine suppository we make with your name on it!

him: YES!

me: ZOMG!

Leave me another message asshole:

timeline. this is last thursday.

8:55am: fax Rx received, fax Rx printed.

9:00am: call to patient made. message left to call us about prescription.

9:15am: message left on our refill request mailbox that they had received our message and were returning our call, but by leaving a message.

9:20am: i return call, and have to leave a message, asking for them to call back and speak to a human

9:22am: another message left on our refill request mailbox that they had received our message and were returning our call, but by leaving another message.

9:25am: i call, it goes to voicemail, i don't leave a message

today, tuesday.

8:55am: retrieving messages from refill request mailbox, it's the person from thursday returning our call again because they hadn't received a message that we received their message.

9:00am: i call, get voicemail, proceed to leave another message asking for them to call and press number 2 to talk to a human when it picks up because leaving a message isn't getting us anywhere.

9:05am: the red light is on the phone indicating there is a refill request message in the refill request mailbox. so i check it, because i hate myself. it's them again. i've decided that this is my life.

9:06am: "hi this is joel leaving you a message letting you know i received your message that you received my message when i left a message about the previous two messages we had left for each other regarding the original message i left regarding the prescription we received for you or a member of your family. if you get this message, please call us back and leave us a message with your credit card information only. your card will be charged an unspecified amount and your suppository will rather be made into an injection and we have decided on a flavor of tuna surprise since we have been unable to communicate with you regarding the specifics of your doctor's order. thanks."

11:22am: phone rings. it's the patient. they're calling about a prescription that was faxed in last thursday.

COME AT ME BRO

Oh, we deliver:

him: hey

me: straw!

him: do you guys deliver?

me: yep. it's just we let UPS or the post office deliver it, and we call it shipping

him: shipping is the same thing as delivery?

me: i'd say so. delivery is normally same day, and shipping tends to be an overnight or over a few nights process, but they both accomplish the same thing.

him: i never thought of it like that

me: you ever had a shipment "delivered"?

him: or a delivery "shipped"!

me & him at the same time: woah.

shipping & delivery.

it's only different if you let it be.

My super hero:

me: so you're at 1234 super grover avenue

him: no, just grover ave

me: you sure the grover isn't super grover?

him: you mean like grover who never uses contractions when he sings?

me: free shipping upon your house sir. free shipping upon your entire family.

I quoted Boyz In The Hood:

him: are you familiar with dr. _____ out of skokie?

me: he the one that collect all them comic books?

him: ...

me: man he got more comic books than a mug.

him: ...

me: sorry, haven't seen boyz in the hood in like a year and i'm starting to quote lil' doughboy all over the place.

him: ...

me: you were saying?

him: i don't even remember why i was calling.

Can I axe you a question?

her: can i ask you a question?

me: you just did

her: i mean a medical question

me: let me put you on hold and grab you a pharmacist

her: nah nah nah, i don't trust those people

me: ME EITHER! especially because i'm related to them and their ancestry can be traced to luxembourg

her: nah, i just dont trust people in white coats

me: well, today one coat is periwinkle and the other is hunter orange

her: hunter orange?

me: yeah, green tie too. dude's living OUT LOUD

her: let me talk to periwinkle

me: excellent choice

Wrong number, bitch:

me: the compounder, this is joel, can i help you?

her: ah, wrong number

me: no problem, bye

two minutes later

me: the compounder, this is joel, can i help you?

same her: ah, number is still wrong

me: i agree! have a good one, bye

three minutes later

me: the compounder, this is joel, can i help you?

same her again: why does this number keep reaching the compounder?

me: what's the number?

her: *reads my phone number back to me*

me: that's our number. it's no wonder you were reaching us by calling us at our number

her: but im trying to call _____

me: i don't know what that is, but let me google

it for you

her: aw thanks! you don't have to do that

me: well we've already talked more on the phone today than i've talked to my wife, so we might as well make the most of it.

her: haha

me: ok google isn't giving me anything for that business, what's the correct spelling?

her: i don't know, im driving

me: if we, as a nation, can't drive and spell at the same time, i fear for our future

her: ...

me: want me to try a different name or...

her: what do you guys do there?

me: we are a compounding pharmacy, so we make everything from scratch. we do flavored animal medicines, hormone replacement creams, injections for multiple sclerosis, autoimmune medications, sterile eyedrops, you name it, and we are also the "suppository repository" of the midwest

her: ok i don't need any of that, but you're a nice person for not hanging up on m-

hang up

don't waste my time bitch, these suppositories
ain't finna moisten themselves

Sweat on the toilet seat:

I couldn't get to the phone fast enough, but I was able to pick it up just before it went to voicemail. this conversation picks up where I picked up.

me: the compounder, this is joel, can I help you?

him: ...of course there's sweat on the toilet seat

me: ...of course.

him: sorry that wasn't meant for you.

me: either way, the idea that a toilet seat wouldn't be sweaty is to assume human skin and plastic don't generate heat when in contact for three to fifteen minutes...

him: exactly, it's like explaining why you're sweating after getting out of the shower me: dude, I sweat for at least 20 minutes after a shower no matter what season it is, my ma used to tell me it's because my body temperature needs to cool down gradually after being under hot water for a few minutes, but I like to tell people it's just because im damn sexy

him: oh I don't doubt you're sexy out of the sho-

me: don't finish that sentence, we don't even know each other yet

him: hey thanks, listen, im calling about a testosterone prescription, are you who I would talk to?

me: he is I and I am him, slim with the tilted brim. SERIAAAALLL KILLAAAAAAA

him: what?

me: nothing, I've just always wanted to quote a snoop dogg song while on the phone with a customer

Upspeak:

him: hi, i needed to pick something up?

me: are you asking me?

him: yes, i need to pick something up?

me: if you're asking for my permission, it is granted

him: okay?

me: i feel like you're asking me a question again. have we dicussed this something that you need to pick up prior to this conversation?

him: yes?

me: you don't sound too sure of yourself

him: i called last week?

me: you did or you think you did?

him: thursday?

me: are you giving me options?

Overcharged:

her: hi, i think i got overcharged for my last prescription

me: aw shuggieduggiequackquack, that's no good, let me take a look

her: thanks

me: *typing and clicking, clicking and typing* it looks like this time you got two months worth of the medication instead of one

her: and?

me: and one month is $48 and two months is $73

her: so you admit you charged me more?

me: um, well. yea. i admit it, yes. did you only want one month?

her: no, i ordered two months worth

me: ok great. well the price you paid for two

months is the price for two months so everything looks good on my end, was there something else i can help you with?

her: i don't find it especially polite of you to charge me double for something without talking with me first

me: you ordered two months of the medication

her: but i had no idea it would be so much money, this is double!

me: double would be $96, but this is $73, which is the price for two months. did you want me to work up a return shipment label to ship back the second month we filled for you on accident and i can issue a refund for the balance? i'm sorry for the inco-

her: no! i ordered two months worth!

me: let me place you on a brief hold so i can stare out my window for a minute

HOLD ON HOLD ON HOLD

me: ok, i've checked with myself and i am at a complete loss for how to rectify the situation other than either charging you the remaining $23 so that it IS double the cost for double the medication, or i can send you a return shipping label and i can refund you for the returned amount, or i can try one other way of explaining it.

her: i ordered two months, i don't want to return anything!

me: ok, let's try this with cheeseburgers. so i got these cheeseburgers. last time you had one. it was $48 and it was delicious. this time, you want two cheeseburgers. most burger places would charge you $96 for two burgers, but because we're saving on the plate by putting both burgers on the same plate, we only charge you $73 for both burgers. you ordered two burgers, received two burgers, technically only paid for 1 and three quarters burgers.

her: that doesn't make any sense.

me: let me place you on a brief hold again so i can stare out my window for a minute...

HOLD ON HOLD ON HOLD

me: ok, i've spoken with my manager me and he says we can give you the same deal for one month that we did last time, but for this most recent time, because we filled your order for two months, that the price for two is going to remain at the two month price. is that okay?

her: i appreciate that.

me: i apologize for the confusion. i'll make a note in your file regarding the discount then.

her: thank you.

me: ***returns to staring out window***

A New Program We're Offering

her: how much is your ___ injection?

me: for one 30ml vial it is $73

her: so it's 70 dollars for a hundred 30ml vials?

me: no. those words did not come out of my mouth, no.

her: so it's 130ml for a 70 dollar vial?

me: no. it's $73 for one invidual vial that contains 30ml of injection

her: how many injections is that? how long will that last?

me: if you are using 1ml daily, it's 30 injections that would last you 30 days. if you are doing a different protocol where it's 1ml 3-4 times a week, it could be as long as 70 days or as short

as 52 days. it all depends on what the doctor
writes the prescription for.

her: so a 30ml vial lasts 30 days if i'm using 1ml
a day?

me: yes. very math.

her: sounds confusing.

me: oh it is, if you let it be.

her: this is all so overwhelming. but your price is
cheaper than the last place i called.

me: well, we are offering a new program where
you pay what you want as long as you pay the
minimum amount of $73 per 30ml vial. so let's
not close doors we haven't opened yet.

her: what?

Please Stop Talking:

her: hi, i'm calling about an order i placed a few weeks ago but haven't received yet and normally you guys are johnny on the spot but i haven't received the order yet so i'm wondering if there's a hold up for some weird reason. i mean, i left the message on your voicemail, at least i hope it was your voicemail, but it's not like you to take this long, so i'm hoping you got my order out and it's just an issue with shipping because like i said, this is not how i normally interact with your pharmacy, you've been very quick the last few times i've ordered and this just doesn't make sense so if you could verify that my order was filled and was already shipped i would greatly appreciate it.

me: *exhales*

her: i placed the order WEEKS ago. is there someone i can talk to regarding the order i placed that still hasn't arrived? i mean, normally i get my order within a few days but this is already bordering on a month, and i just don't know what could've happened. can you look me up in your computer? i mean, the mail shouldn't take a month from where you are to where i am, this is a bit ridiculous.

me: who a-

her: isn't there a computer program where you can look me up by my name? i don't have the prescription number because i've been out of it for so long. also, the last order i got was smaller than the first order i got, but whatever. can you find me in your system?

me: please stop talking.

her: i mea-, what?

me: please stop talking.

her: ok.

me: please state your name slowly.

her: FIRST NAME. LAST NAME. i should be in

your computer as i've ordered from you a number of times. this is the first time i've ever had an issue with your pharmacy because normally you guys are super fast but this time it's just not what i expected. I'm just surprised no one has called to check and see if i've received my ord-

PLACES CALL ON HOLD

HOLDS HEAD IN HANDS

THIS IS MY LIFE NOW

CRIES THE TEARS OF A THOUSAND CRIES

Thanks for reading!

You're the breast!

For more information on **The Compounder** visit www.thecompounder.com

For more information on **Joel Frieders** visit www.google.com and type in *"Joel Frieders"*

For more information **Jose Garibaldi** visit www.josegaribaldi.com

CPSIA information can be obtained at www.ICGtesting.com
Printed in the USA
LVOW11s0552120516

487896LV00001B/1/P